There Are Three

Also by Donald Revell

Beautiful Shirt (1994)

Erasures (1992)

New Dark Ages (1990)

The Gaza of Winter (1988)

From the Abandoned Cities (1983)

TRANSLATION:

Alcools by Guillaume Apollinaire (1995)

There Are Three

POEMS BY

Donald Revell

❧

Wesleyan University Press

PUBLISHED BY UNIVERSITY PRESS OF NEW ENGLAND

HANOVER AND LONDON

Wesleyan University Press
Published by University Press of New England, Hanover, NH 03755
© 1998 by Donald Revell
All rights reserved
Printed in the United States of America
5 4 3 2 1
CIP data appear at the end of the book

ACKNOWLEDGMENTS

The author wishes to thank the editors of the following journals, which offered many of these poems their first publication: *American Letters & Commentary, American Poetry Review, Antaeus, Boston Review, Colorado Review, Columbia: A Magazine of Poetry and Prose, Conjunctions, Kenyon Review, New American Writing, No Roses Review, Ohio Review, Partisan Review, SFSU Review, Southwest Review*, and *Volt*.

"There Are Three" also appeared in *The Gertrude Stein Awards in Innovative American Poetry: 1994–1995*, published by Sun & Moon Press.

In addition, the author thanks The National Endowment for the Arts for a fellowship that helped to make the completion of this book possible.

to Benjamin Brecht Revell

Contents

There Are Three

❧ *A Branch of the Discipline*

The red forest is
eager to be seen.
The red fragrance
travels a great distance,
meaning nothing in
general, but in
particular fatal
and entirely personal.

The soul at present
matters less than
instinct, its
later instrument.
Of the 47 nesting
herons displaced
by recent storms,
47 died.

The red forest maintains
perfect silence, eager
to be seen without
distraction. In clear
heavens of destruction
it aborts the unspoken
words so easy to defy.
The soul is a nest.

The soul catches the wind
between numerals. Once
I was eager to remain outside

forever, and once I did.
The future bent
the boughs to breaking.
They cracked silently,
one last thing.

❧ *Overthrow*

I.

On such a night, the stars could not consent to constellations.

My ambition was
at once to stop
dreaming and begin
to sleep, to make
a clear distinction
between the ache
of privation
and cold surfeits
of black sleep.

A calf defecating onto the sleeping head of another calf
instructed me the useless distinction intervening a desert
of joy a desert of defilement. It was no dream. On such a
night, the stars pour down soil through their names.

My ambition was
at once to stop
the river upstanding
the open sea refusing
all surfeits.

2.

Remember unequivocally the instance of mercy,
never prayer. The grammar makes deep channels
and useful islands, the overthrow of swimmers
recurring, undisguised. Mercy remains aloft.

Afterwards will
be nothing to pray.
The broad wake
of so many drowned,
weightless but heavy
with downdraft, did
not say words.

The sum of their pains in pain no more upon the world
undressed all sums. And into all such nakedness hurry
the prayerful, quick to flaw what does not make reply.

On such a night
I saw an earth
above the earth so
long as there was light
until it was gone.

3.

Two alone beside a park:
one is the art school.
Two alone and then a playfield:
one is my hotel.

When the light was gone and the grammar of the congregation
grew accustomed to darkness, only then could the renovation
of sums, nakedness and mercy excel the ocean.

Couples undress in their hotels.
One alone undresses in the art school.
A surplus of privation
renovates the sex of each
into the earth of all.

Night nevertheless. Consenting if amazed, I dreamed a dream
of flying, a haphazard innocence impossible to divide among
the agonies of surface and the soils of the unecstatic air.

Ambition is disgrace.
Although I could not pray,
I chose to pray badly.
Of course it was ugly.

4.

Ambition inquired,
are you the martyred
ocean or infrequent rain?
Of course it was ugly.

Of course my savior
was weathered by rain.
What remains of the crucifix
is a grinning spoon.

Very soon now, the untethered reason of John Calvin
will roam at large in beautiful cities and kill men.

Undressed in a hotel
in Holland the naked vowels
in black and black pallor
copulate like seaways.

Undressed in the art school
in Amsterdam and inwardly
the martyr howls.
She is teeming, inwardly.

An unlikely Puritan likewise howls for her.

5.

At dawn my nature,
remarkable bird
tethered amid predators,
alarmed my loving.

On such a morning
decline is lofty.
Teeming inwardly,
consenting to nothing,

the calf wakes,
ambition wakes,
the insensible swimmer
breaks the air.

Inspired is no way in.
Prayer and uniformity
are no way.
In each in daylight

a desert intervenes,
and then a dream divides
the night following
into white designs.

❧ *Upon Diagnosis*

Being so fast, the things
of this world cling
always to excitement,
seldom or never
to one another.
Pathos is ravishment
by gravity. Myth is monsters
clinging to moments.

To the splendid encampment
Achilles summoned monsters.
Not one arrived, nor
plain nor particular.
Myth is the disappointment
of heroes. Nature
is likewise a disfigurement
of women and men.

I see a shadow meant
for someone else becoming
mine. I hear a blunt
inhuman sound becoming
sharply human. I want
attachment
to literally everything
elemental so everlasting.

❧ *Inquire*

The god is how many
bridges and automobiles
cut off mid-sentence
in the effect of style?

Weak and eerie with
distance like all
magic, scattered,
commingled and gone,

the god persists in
the singing before
the syringes of waking.
He is the pause endlessly.

He breaks the tree,
and it waits to fall.

❧ Societies Can Be Improved.
Societies Cannot Be Good.

an eye open
if and when
23 May 1810
I found the
word golden
an eye open including a self-portrait
thus early thus alone abstraction not
mythologies

and so in Europe now the young women
pay very well to wear bluejeans made
in American prisons by men convicted
of crime early and abstraction alone
cannot compass the mythology driving

an eye open
23 May 1810
I found the
word golden

Blake you should be alive at this hour

Homage to Mrs. Jane Lead

Elsewhere, my animal
is unnatural.
On the paradisal
Street of the Balloon Game,
he is reviled.

In courtyards made
only of vowels
and a little sunlight,
sometimes a fountain,
he is reviled.

In atmospheres
of inverted seedlings,
upended futures,
lovely heads,
he is reviled.

Where the green treaty
sanctifies love,
and the fixed festival
sanctifies the water-hole,
he is reviled.

My animal dies of shame
and representation
ever established among us
in the seedbed of a calculus
none can see.

❧ *Elegy*

myself the other
winter even more
myself the other
still as obscure
a milk white one
a coal black one
winter even more

❧ *Above*

brutally represented
as themselves and so
becoming oceanic too
fast vinery bowls of
surface the surfaces
outfit the wind with
hunters beasts heads
of braids of hair so
brutally white shade
not helpless hunting

✣ My Father

as I remember
an old notion
of floor plan
the gaudy 5 &
10 is nearest
calls to mind
the beginning
the low aisle
and uniformed
exchanges red
sums red ones

❧ *There Are Three*

The moment advances
an illusion that high
sounds perish leaving
illusion free to survive.
This is silence.

An hour along
the groundless tangents
of a meadow is not wasted
until it ends. I feel
the world the less
the more it shows.
This is a picture.

My life disordered itself
amply in chronology
and voices of wolves.
No more voices!
This is a tune.

❧ *To the Lord Protector*

I.

It is incredible
how cold, how far
from all feeling
the spur feels.

Me next. In the middle
way of scarecrow and
imagination, I do not
wonder. I do not open.

Against intelligible flame,
against the goad,
the craving for piety,
God established the body.

The shifting flaws of human permission made it move.

2.

Cruel to remain
in solace, such
a house whose
sound cannot consist
of humanness.

The table is
hazardous. The door
is accidental.
Loneliness never
welcomes echoes.

I taste it sharply.
As it dreams
to happen, sharp
I taste it.
I clash and conjecture.

A thing of stone is not a continuity.

3.

Many find immediate
rest and human things
exempt from harm.
Seeds and sparkles
all blaze again.

But even a famous
man may not
oblige jailers,
so wild a race
has superstition run.

If any two
tasted once
remedy for loneliness,
calamity remains.
Laws are imposed.

Cure of disease crept into the best part of human society.

4.

I trust to protect
tables, astronomy,
and the unconjugal
mind not to suffer.

Words declare
no expression.
Mind hangs off,
closing proportion.

Preposterous
to have made
provisions
while I dreamed.

Soul's lawful contentment is only the fountain.

5.

A discreet man
in wild affections
remains more alone.

More deeply rooted
in other burning
in rational burning

he honors himself
to understand himself
and be considered.

The least grain
is well enough.
Many are married.

God does not principally take care of such cattle.

6.

To end the question
men may often
borrow compulsion
from a snare.

Exhortation is angels.
Compulsion is devils.
One hides, one
bares the claws.

I saw the least sinew
of my body washed
and salted. I saw
it seeking.

The obscene evidence of the question never changed.

7. (DEDICATION)

This day will be
remarkable
or my last.
Like a beast,
I am content
and mutable,
perhaps free.

A few and easy
things, a few words
unearthed in season
revive the ruined
man on earth.
The effortless rainbow
deepens.

My author sang and was deep in her showing.

❧ A Cold September

Means wither. Then
by darker means
late he exits
onto the roads
into the rainy
lines and branches.
His lights are
what he sees.

❧ A New October

energies long and poor
              dawbed
              black and yellow

black freely
ultramarine rarely

nevertheless we come to a deep pure lake

savage   enough
pilgrimage   enough

                  even to the edgewater

like physical pain in beautiful surroundings

apparently dreaming
under a hawk's bough

Extinction

usually unheard

                    it is so common

needing only a few

                    more words or one

success you cannot dispose of it

                              by listening to it

and so a difference

                    in cultures in the case of men

cannot dispose of it

                    only changes the weeds

and emphasis

                    of the cold wildflowers

living a few more days

❧ *Thanksgiving for a Son*

sudden fever stills

                           his small permission

[quiet roseate
[quiet roseate

                 quiet German village inside

a child's presage

❧ *Advent*

The wind that shows a city
fills an iris, also
a heart suspended without wires
in the sparse lighting.

On a winter morning,
homelessness rides an impossible
animal into impossible vineyards.
The next wind shows a city

suspended in each vine, also
hanging the man.
If the hour had moved
without wires or the sparse

lighting above the wind,
none was hanged. Snow
fed the animals. Their eyes
we named for flowers also.

❧ A Clasp

Below the shapeliness
of every hand
exposed in error
of the hand's strength
ache the usual
ligature and tendon
inflamed by injustice
made, allowed.

At Epiphany, hand-
made civil traffic
steals through town.
Hilarious and undemocratic
is every miracle. Ache
and error, ache and
correction strive as usual,
unshaped in the disguise of angels.

❧ *Once Divided*

In prayer, the open hand
collapses. The surface
of the lake is nearly
ice, and even without
it the wind destroys
silence in the only tree.

In my open hand, winter
eludes the exact center.
On shore, the heron is ice.
In flight, the heron is
a cloud between the lake
and a crescent moon.

The water does not freeze.
The moon withdraws into
the frozen air. Something
exactly mine arises
in like efforts and lake-
effects and dies there.

❧ Scherzo

I.

Snowfall narrows the streets and sky.
Overnight, many fires changed the air
to something close and homely.
Light alone at the surface of light
sparkles, equable everywhere.
In the spree of men's eyes and calendars
duration appears white. The soul
of duration is white also.

Almost nothing
but sensations cross
the surface spree
of streets and sky.
Rousseau: "My
ideas are nothing but sensations now."
Many fires
change exactly so.

Even the smoke
of almost featureless houses
sustains
music of variation
beginning in my childhood
every cold morning.

Rousseau: "The earth
of my understanding
is alone."

Of equal loneliness
light sparkles
winter durations
like the death of souls,

having noted all such memorable flowers.

2.

A winter street
at an early hour
is not stranger.
It is something added.

My soul rejoices and goes.
Thoreau: "The snow is made by
enthusiasm. I see no sabbath."

Immersion or
approach, it
makes a difference.
Death apart or
memory alone, it
makes a difference.

Every morning, beginning in childhood,
the music of variation sustains
the equal loneliness of every soul.

I approached my father.
I was immersed in my father.
In the early hours of his death
hair all over my body was like snow.

Thoreau: "The dog explodes
his alphabet better
than savages."
I see no sabbath, only
a stranger returning.

Claudia returns with news
of the first flowers,
ever the same but lately
unimaginable,

ice taking the full measure of blaze.

3.

Noise of arrival
allows the winter
a little while longer
like a sieve like childhood.
Still early but unstill
the street grows wild.

Rousseau: "My hope
is in danger of starlings."

Something I trusted
apart from solitude
died with my father
o worse than lonely

A savage making laces and dictionaries
explodes his alphabet.
More slowly, the first flowers
pronounce a duration, music in
danger of starlings, worse than lonely.

Rousseau: "My imagination is so
much noise." The full measure
of blaze, my soul's portion,
speeds the news.
I am death. And so are you

Unimaginable music changing changes nothing.
Children arriving indoors early
from the snow with fists of flowers
imagine the world has changed, but only
music changes. The duration of flowers
is always smoke. My soul makes a fist and goes
apart among strangers, unequal to the least

movement of the lowest branches in the trees.

4.

At least upward, at least the earth cascades
into a sparrow's nest, becoming wide.
My soul has made a fist. The street has made
an imagination of flowers shrouded
in daylight. Riot and arrival move
low branch, higher branch, four elements and five.

Like a sieve or like childhood narrowing
into a father's death, the street is alive
all right, increasing all right, but not changing.
Nothing added music to the snow.

Thoreau: "To the innocent there are no
angels. Wrecks of meadows fill the coves."

Thoreau: "I saw a caterpillar crawling
on the snow. The past cannot be presented."

Thoreau: "I am not penitent. God prefers
I approach not penitent but forgetful."

My piety
nested a while.

At least earth if
no angel schemed for me.

Earth schemes apart.

An imagination of flowers shrouded in daylight
riots and arrives. Speed, my soul,
such news, and quiet my father. No further
music survives in snow. Unequal
winter becomes smoke cascading
into the street. It increases. Thoreau:
"God schemes for me." A further music
forgets the flowers even as they bloom.

5.

As pain
and delightedness contend in a sick child,
a scherzo of destiny and flowers
contends in the ground, in the least upward
narrowness of street and sky. It opposes
piety to outrage, penitence
to the sheer speed of human souls.

Rousseau: "In order to please my dog, I
made a plan. The better prayer is mine."

My soul is alive all right, but nothing
to do with me. The street is greener
since I began, no thanks to me, no thanks
to any sacrifice imagined or made.
Unimaginable changes nested a while
under cover of increase and then arose.
My father died. Claudia brought in flowers.
A scherzo of durations and departures
sped the news of worse than lonely-o.

Rousseau: "I let them yelp."

To hound by underhand,
honor and pulverize.
To pay homage,
proceed at haphazard.
The better prayer
is also mine.

Beginning in childhood
light sparkled and flowers
fisted their beautiful
contentions without choice,

only pain and delightedness.

Beloved has found
unseen illustrations
of other situations.
The need to change
rivals the sun.
At least as far
as the nearest mountain
Beloved has found
a fineness still unseen.
Today is fine.
Tomorrow is fine.
With peril through a mountain
Beloved has found
in variation
a last religion.
Stupefied with agreement
it rivals the sun.

The Memory of New England

scarce American pamphlet

                    like a stream or pencil of sweet light

surviving in solitude

                triumphed in a solitude God himself

is not above the possibility

                  is not above the permissions

and in floods and waterspouts

                   came tenderness they said

the cattle and even everybody seemed changed

❧ *Hypethral*

flowering skullcap here

          as there I lived in a halo

the place deserves a name

          the slow [wreath]

of circus horses expressive

          as it flows off

~~their American color~~

          I have drunk an arrowhead

deserves to be called

          August ideally

that would be fun alive

          the tigir's musical smile

that would be a sunny day

❧ *A Day of Crisis No a Quiet Day*

cloud shapes of infants
sprawl where luckily
for all this summer
is one receding fabric
of exchanges abstract
and hot a solstice
and anniversary of life
for death though each
remains alive forever
for a few no matter
each remains alive

❧ Outbreak

(variations on the testimony and excommunication of
Anne Hutchinson, Massachusetts Bay Colony, 1637–1638)

I.

Given to sweet motion
the wilderness believes
one fair one of flowers
to be a moral blossom.
We go so far. Walks now,
only legend remaining.

"I came afterwards to the window when you was writing."

But in their documents
her judges had written
    "Insolent."

In its branches
spirit shelters
air with wailing.
The air thunders
unavailingly there.

"Fear is a snare. Why should I be afraid."

    If I was in error
    but not mistaken,
    if my glass was gone
    but not broken
      (*defaced*)

2.

My path illuminates
all the interior of
a dusky mirror, the
left shoulder higher
than the right is in
memory's intricate.

We must study distinctions aftertimes will adore.
If the glass be taken away, we shall see more.

God is going. Walks now, only God remaining.

                    (*wanting*)
an immediate promise He will deliver them
(*wanting*)   in a day of trouble

These emotions she retained
in the universal heart, in
a new eye: rational charity
                active piety
                appearing as blindness appears
                in the face in bright sunlight
                exactly like a smile.

3.

"Here is a great stir about graces
and looking to hearts, but give me
Christ. Tell me not of meditations
and duties, but tell me of Christ."

Christ is one thing. The soul is another
the wild outskirt
of the earth will
prove the ruin of.

And mischief, the poor babe, grew in the forest.
                              (*defaced*)

A stick a bunch of rags a flower
need no transformation. The hour
given to sweet motion is a soul.

I came to the window when God was going.
In low condition,
little number and
remoteness things

                    outbreaks of temper
                    had a kind of value
                    and even a comfort.

4.

A memory a promise or a flower sheared away
was not made
                    but taken from a bush of wild roses.
Seeing them, she began to cry out for a red rose.

"God has left me to distinguish
between the voice of my Beloved
and John Baptist and Antichrist."

But daybreak unites what belongs together,
and there are two kinds of distinction.
There are (*something wanting*)

"What he declares he does not know himself."

I know a day of small
and a day of infancy.
At the window vividly
just now and entirely
inarticulate the form
given to sweet motion

broke apart and
               there's colors all
kinds all round.

5.

Of realities surrounding us,
their pith and substance was
                  wasted
                  wronged
                  misplaced.

"I desire to speak to our teacher."

                  In a state of desire,
                  what belongs together
                  ignores the barriers.

Daybreak
have you
any word
your own
or I one
fair one
remaining?

God is gone, only a window and a wilderness
remaining, not made but taken,
thinnest fantasy of beginnings

taken from a bush of wild red roses.

No Difference I Know They Are

more of a red heart

               the powder man wants

the red-hearted the poor wood

                    has the aspen any?

greater use give me

               gladness which has never given place

give me names

             for the rivers of Hell but none

for the rivers of Heaven

               this day

there is no paint like the air

               this day

is a godsend to the wasps

UNIVERSITY PRESS OF NEW ENGLAND publishes books under its
own imprint and is the publisher for Brandeis University Press,
Dartmouth College, Middlebury College Press, University of New
Hampshire, Tufts University, and Wesleyan University Press.

ABOUT THE AUTHOR
Donald Revell was a National Poetry Series winner in 1982 for his first
book of poems, *From the Abandoned Cities,* and won a Pushcart Prize in
1985. His collection *New Dark Ages* (Wesleyan, 1990), won the PEN
Center USA West Award for Poetry. He is currently Professor of
English at the University of Utah, Salt Lake City. His other books in-
clude *Erasures* (Wesleyan, 1992) and *Beautiful Shirt* (Wesleyan, 1994); he
also translated a volume of poetry by Guillaume Apollinaire, entitled
Alcools (Wesleyan, 1995).

LIBRARY OF CONGRESS CATALOGING-IN-PUBLICATION DATA
Revell, Donald, 1954–
    There are three : poems / by Donald Revell.
        p.   cm. — (Wesleyan poetry)
    ISBN 0–8195–2246–5 (alk. paper). —
    ISBN 0–8195–2247–3 (pbk. : alk. paper)
    I. Title.   II. Series
PS3568.E793T44   1998
811'.54—dc21   98–16359